MW00989671

Civilizing
the City Dog

A Guide to Rehabilitating Aggressive
Dogs in an Urban Environment

Pamela S. Dennison
with Jolanta Benal

Supplement to
How to Right a Dog Gone Wrong

Alpine
PUBLICATIONS
Crawford, CO

Civilizing the City Dog

A guide to rehabilitating aggressive dogs in an urban environment

Supplement to *How to Right a Dog Gone Wrong*

ISBN 978-1-57779-089-1

Cataloging-in-Publication Data

Dennison, Pamela.
  Civilizing the city dog : a guide to rehabilitating aggressive dogs in an urban environment : supplement to How to right a dog gone wrong / Pamela S. Dennison, with Jolanta Benal.
    p. cm.
  ISBN 978-1-57779-089-1 (pb)
  1. Dogs–Training. 2. Dogs–Behavior. 3. Aggressive behavior in animals. I. Benal, Jolanta, 1958- II. Dennison, Pamela. How to right a dog gone wrong. III. Title.

SF431.D4454 2007
636.088'7–dc22   2007030544

The information contained in this book is complete and accurate to the best of our knowledge. All recommendations are made without guarantee on the part of the author or Alpine Publications, Inc. The author and publisher disclaim any liability with the use of this information.

For the sake of simplicity, the terms " he" or "she" are sometimes used to identify an animal or person. These are used in the generic sense only. No discrimination of any kind is intended toward either sex.

Many manufacturers secure trademark rights for their products. When Alpine Publications is aware of a trademark claim, we identify the product name by using initial capital letters.

Design and Layout: Laura Newport
Editing: Deborah Helmers
Photographs: All photos by the author unless otherwise indicated.

1 2 3 4 5 6 7 8 9 0

Printed in the United States of America.

TABLE OF CONTENTS

✲ *Preparing Yourself* ✲ *Riding Shotgun*
✲ *Escape Routes and Props* ✲ *Vet Visits* ✲ *Flexibility*
✲ *Neighbors and Advisors* ✲ *When You Are Being Reasonable and
"They" Are Not* ✲ *Potty Breaks*

✲ *Start Indoors* ✲ *Round Robin a Plus* ✲ *Whistle Training*
✲ *Stays and Self-Control* ✲ *Rev Up and Cool Down* ✲ *Scent Games*
✲ *Free Shaping* ✲ Lie Down on a Mat ✲ Wipe Your Feet
✲ Nose Targeting and More ✲ *Staying Motivated*
✲ *No Time to Train* ✲ *Relaxing*

✲ *Changing the Meaning of Signals* ✲ *Doorbell and Elevator Cues*
✲ Doorbell Ring ✲ Elevator Ding! ✲ *Breaking It Down*
✲ *Where's the Dog?* ✲ *Get Out of Dodge*

✲ *Muzzles: Pros and Cons* ✲ *Training Tips* ✲ *The Mechanics*
✲ *Attention Heeling* ✲ *Loose-Leash Walking*
✲ *Change of Direction Cue* ✲ *Troubleshooting*

✲ *Damage Control I: When You Can't Escape and Your Dog Goes Over
Threshold* ✲ *Damage Control II: When Real Catastrophe Strikes*

Dedicated to you, the urban dweller, who, despite all odds, go that extra mile to help your dog.

ACKNOWLEDGMENTS

Pam Dennison:

Thanks go to the IAABC (International Association of Animal Behavior Consultants) and Kathi O'Malley for inviting me to be the first presenter in the new Guided Study Program for continuing education credits. Without that opportunity I never would have realized just how many people live in a big city with aggressive or reactive dogs.

During my time on the list, someone asked a specific question about desensitization in a city, and I didn't know the answer. Jolanta Benal wrote a wonderful response and the rest is history! That e-mail of Jolanta's gave me the idea for writing this supplement. In one of our communications, one comment of hers really hit home:"It's not an option to do the dry runs and just not walk the dog for a few days. It's the single City Reality Point that makes us urban folks throw the book against the wall while screaming 'BUT I CAN'T DO THAT!!!!!'" She has been gracious enough to help me modify many of the exercises in this book to better suit my city "cousins" and better help their dogs. Jolanta also opened my eyes to the many issues that face owners of reactive and aggressive dogs living in a more urban environment.

To my ever-present students and friends who so willingly and repeatedly subject themselves to my photo sessions: you ladies are the best! The really neat thing is that all of these dogs (except Takoda and Beau) are in reality reactive or aggressive, and not one of them had any issues during the photo session! Not even Gus (the dog leaping up in the air) who "seemingly" went wild lunging at Sally—they actually like each other.

Karen Carroll and her two Rottweilers, Esmonds Takoda's Good Medicine CGC (Takoda) and Deerwood's Just a Gigolo RA, AOP, NJP, HIC, APDT RL1, RL2, RL3 (Jerome).

Jane Killion and her Bull Terrier, Ch. Corsaire Carpe Diem of Madcap, VA, NAP, NJP, NAC, RL2, TT, CGC (Ruby).

Gina Boderck and her All-American, Gus.

Kitt Allan and her Mini Australian Shepherd, Georgie.

Cecilia Castillo and her Border Collie mix.

Sally and her Border Collie, Whisper (who graces the cover of this book).

Deborah Rubin and her Belgian Tervuren, Echo.

And of course, my own boys, ARCH Ewe Are Beyond a Shadow of a Doubt, CGC, A-CD, NA, NAJ, RL3, TSW (Shadow) and ARCH Surely Ewe Beau Jest, CGC, TDI, CD, A-CD, NAP, NAJP, RL3, TSW (Beau).

And as always, many thanks and appreciation goes to my agent and friend, Jacky Sach of Bookends, LLC, and to Deborah Helmers, editor extraordinaire.

Jolanta Benal:

I'm especially grateful to Pam Dennison, not only for the opportunity to work with her on this project but also for the original *How to Right a Dog Gone Wrong*, which was a great help to me and my dog-aggressive dog. Pam gets scads of extra credit for genuinely and thoughtfully responding to the special challenges faced by city dogs and their people, challenges that non-urban trainers sometimes dismiss. I believe that her book will be one my fellow city dwellers don't feel the need to throw against the wall.

Warm thanks to Polly Hanson and Barbara Giella, my friends and my first mentors in clicker training, and to trainers Viviane Arzoumanian and Marion Weiner for their friendship and their help with the material for this book. Thanks and love to Sarah Egan for years of pro-dog propaganda, and the same to three great teacher dogs: Isabella, Muggsy Malone, and Juniper.

INTRODUCTION

··

In *How to Right a Dog Gone Wrong,* my first book on rehabili-tating aggressive dogs, I outlined the training that I use in my local New Jersey area. After writing it, however, I became aware that many people with aggressive or reactive dogs live in densely populated areas and therefore have more specialized needs than those of us liv-ing in more rural places. Many of the behaviors mentioned or taught in *How to Right a Dog Gone Wrong,* as well as many of the proto-cols, might seem to be impossible to train while living in a city.

What follows is a supplement to *How to Right a Dog Gone Wrong.* I will not be repeating what is in the first book, but aug-menting and changing some of the procedures to better fit the needs of those living in urban areas. So if you don't yet have a copy of *How to Right a Dog Gone Wrong,* you will need to get one.

In a city you will often find it impossible to set up safe situations and create enough space between your dog and his provoking stim-uli. This book will help you work around those limitations to gain the control, calmness, and success that you need with your aggressive or reactive dog. You will also encounter situations unique to the urban setting, unknown to your more rural counterparts. I have added exer-cises and ideas that address some of those issues.

I used to think that every dog could be turned around. However, the more I work with aggressive/reactive dogs, the less I believe it. A city's unpredictable environment, when combined with the intensity of a particular dog's response, the number of his triggers, and other factors such as the size and age of the dog, may very well reach a crit-ical point—a point at which rehabilitation in another context might be possible but in the city simply cannot be achieved.

I *hate* this—I wish fervently that there was hope for every dog. Sometimes the dog is just so damaged and the "real world" he lives in cannot possibly accommodate his enormous needs. There is an outer limit to workability—if you have a 120-pound dog that is severely human-aggressive and you live on the 10th floor of a high-rise, the reality is that nothing will help you work with your dog. You need to either move or euthanize the dog. There is a lot you can do to help repair your dog even if you live in a big city, but there are real limits as well. The severity of your dog's behavior problems, combined with the limited extent to which you can control the circumstances, may cause the whole thing to become unworkable in terms of real change in your dog and safety for others.

We don't like to hear this. We love our dogs, inappropriate behavior notwithstanding. The decision to euthanize for any reason never comes easily and never comes without regret for what might have been had this or that been different.

However, for many dogs, most of the time, remarkable improvements *are* possible. Even if your dog-reactive dog sometimes runs headfirst into another dog coming around the corner. Even if your human-reactive dog can't always be prevented from seeing and hearing people walk by. Even if you don't dare take the elevator in your apartment building lest someone else get on. Even if your dog-aggressive dog is attacked by a dog that lives around the corner from you and is always off leash. Yes, improvements will come more slowly than they would if you lived in a more rural area, and setbacks will be more frequent. But the improvements really can happen. Patience, ingenuity, and being able to think and react fast will become your best tools.

City Basics

PREPARING YOURSELF

In what I will call "The Big Book" (*How to Right a Dog Gone Wrong: A Roadmap for Rehabilitating Aggressive Dogs*), I talk a great deal in Chapter Three about handling your own stress when out with your dog. Positive mental imagery, finding your "safe place," and belly breathing are all very important. However, those of you who live in a big city may well need to take stress reduction a few steps further. Once you have practiced in the safety of your living room, take a dog walk *without* your dog. Really pretend that your dog is with you and take a walk, noticing exactly where the trouble spots and safety zones are, and work on breathing and being calm. I know this sounds silly, but do it anyway: hold on to a leash to get the feel of it in your hand so that the entire scenario is real (just add dog).

Once you are done with that first walk, go home and re-live the experience in your head. Visualize it in exacting detail. While you are doing so, practice the Big Three (positive mental imagery, finding your safe place, and belly breathing). Picture problem scenarios (for

Don't panic! I know it isn't an option to keep your dog locked up in your house or apartment until you are ready mentally. This issue will be discussed later on in this chapter.

instance, a skateboarder coming around the corner at you), and plan how you can best handle them using the tools in this book. If there's a place you can't avoid that historically presents difficulties for your dog, plan for it and visualize yourself carrying out that plan to minimize outbursts from your dog. Continue until your heart rate can remain normal throughout your visualized walk.

Go out for a second walk (also without your dog) and actually move into those problem zones as if your dog were with you, all the while practicing the Big Three. Those of you who do agility or have been to an agility trial have seen the competitors walk the course. These people make weird hand movements and talk to and even praise their imaginary dogs (guilty as charged) in order to imprint the entire course in their heads, so they will know how to navigate it to their best advantage when it is their turn. I want you to build up to where you too are "walking the course," building up some confidence and muscle and brain memory, so that when you actually have your dog with you, you will know what to do. Practice these walks without your dog as often as you can, and you will start to see a difference in his behavior when you do have him with you.

When you're taking a reactive/aggressive dog out in public, a huge source of anxiety may be the feeling that you're not in control of the situation. Provoking stimuli can leap out at you at any moment, and you may fear the result will be catastrophic—both emotionally and/or physically for you or your dog. Here are some points to remember that may help you.

- ❖ Your role, when you're out with your difficult dog, is to protect him, others, and yourself. You're the mama bear. Work to be cool and calm for your dog even if it's difficult to do so for yourself. Fake it till you make it!
- ❖ The more information you amass—information about where and when your dog's triggers are likely to appear and a detailed understanding of his threshold levels for reacting to various stimuli—the less likely you are to be blindsided.
- ❖ The more you practice your dog's foundation skills and the better you become at using the landscape to escape problem

situations or to keep your dog below threshold in the first place, the bigger your "bank account" of successes will grow, and the less you'll have to fear from unexpected encounters.

❖ A setback is just that, a setback; it's not the end of the world.

❖ Most of you can take steps to make real tragedy exceedingly unlikely. You can keep your dog on leash, muzzle him if need be, use your awareness of the environment, and hone your skills to keep out of serious trouble.

❖ Some of you may encounter unfortunate situations in your day-to-day lives. You may be harassed and humiliated, with strangers telling you to euthanize your dog or "just give him a good correction." You may run into people who imply that your dog's aggression reflects your own personality problems (or you may feel that is what they are thinking).

In the Big Book, I spoke a great deal about denial. Acknowledge your fears, put them into words, and remind yourself that you can cope with them because you are taking appropriate steps to work on your dog's problems.

RIDING SHOTGUN

Let me preface "riding shotgun" with a disclaimer: I understand this tactic may not be feasible for you. The cost may be too high or you may not have anyone to help you. As with any of the exercises in this book, take what works for you, or adapt these tools and suggestions to better suit your own specific needs. Improvisation is an important skill for working with reactive and aggressive dogs in your environment.

Whether or not you and your dog are ready or however far along he is in his training, you probably *must* take your dog outside—at the very least, to potty. In the beginning, I recommend having someone come with you, both when you have your dog with you and when you don't. You can practice remaining calm because you'll have someone there helping you. If your dog is human-aggressive, be sure to have someone help you who your dog likes. If he is dog–aggressive, your choice of helper is unlimited. Two pairs of eyes are better than one. Your helper can let you know when there's a bike rider at two o'clock or a dog walker coming up behind you with five dogs, and you can act accordingly.

If you are having a hard time finding a friend or relative with the same schedule as you to come with you, by all means hire a pet sitter, dog walker, or some older kid down the block to help you.

Make sure you apprise your helper of what kinds of provoking stimuli to watch for and make sure he or she understands the need to scan all 360 degrees—not just to the right or left. Teach your helper how to split between your dog and provoking stimuli. You won't need the friend forever—just for a short time until you can go it alone.

Cecilia is riding shotgun, splitting while I feed Shadow. I call this move "Elvis is leaving the building." Photo by Gina Boderck.

If you can't find anyone to ride shotgun, I still want you to plot out your walk, complete with escape routes. If necessary, at first take your dog out only to relieve himself. Be sure to provide plenty of mental stimulation indoors, especially by practicing the foundation behaviors listed in Chapters Seven and Eight in the Big Book. If he is toy motivated, play with him while on your walk to keep him busy. If he is food motivated, go ahead and feed continuously as you walk. Do what it takes to keep your dog below threshold for reactivity.

Because physically and mentally tiring your dog outside may be impossible in the beginning, indoor exercise for dogs living in the Big City is discussed in Chapter Two.

Cecilia is using a toy to keep Whisper occupied while navigating her route. Note that Cecilia began using the toy before she needed it and that she also is keeping an eye on the person walking past.

Kitt is using a mailbox as an escape route for Georgie.

Cecilia is using an umbrella as a sight barrier for Sally.

ESCAPE ROUTES AND PROPS

Escape routes in the Big City can be quite challenging to find, recognize instantly, and utilize. Simple objects, such as garbage cans, Dumpsters, parked cars, shrubbery, benches, telephone poles, vestibules, mailboxes, bus stop shelters with posters on them, sides of steps at front porches, and alleyways can all be used as visual barriers

Jane is stretching to see over of the top of the shrubbery...

...and then races behind it with Ruby to let the walkers go past.

or to provide sufficient distance to keep your dog calm. Some, like parked cars, are almost always available; others, like Dumpsters, come and go unpredictably. The break in the hedgerow at the park is likely to stay where it is all of the time, but a vestibule may be locked, or people and/or dogs may be using it. Most of the time you'll be walking in familiar places, which means that you'll soon have a mental inventory of your hot spots and sanctuaries.

Kitt is using this alleyway as an escape route to wait until the dog and pedestrian traffic pass by.

Kitt is using the traffic-light pole as a safety net and is feeding Georgie while waiting for the pedestrian traffic to pass.

Other possibilities for barriers: an opened umbrella, a shoulder bag, or large portfolio-type bag. (You may have to desensitize your dog to these, of course.) Be creative!

When walking Shadow off leash on the trail, I learned that if I attached the leash when I saw someone coming, Shadow would get very nervous (even if I was breathing calmly). He wasn't aggressing, but he was clearly linking the leash with "provoking stimuli coming." The act of putting the leash on during a walk became a cue that something scary was coming down the pike. To undo this association, I began to attach the leash when no one was coming; we'd walk a little bit; and then I'd take the leash off again.

The moral of this story is that you should zip into a safety zone even when nothing scary is coming toward you so that act doesn't begin predicting the appearance of triggers. If your dog sees racing behind a car or behind some shrubbery as an antecedent of getting Vienna sausages instead of something to be afraid of, so much the better.

VET VISITS

You don't need this book to tell you that getting in and out of the vet's office is a particular challenge for urban owners of reactive and aggressive dogs. No parking lot for you to wait in, maybe no car either, a postage-stamp-size waiting room, and a crowded sidewalk out front—all these are serious issues for you.

Chances are, the vet's office staff will be very happy to help you work out a way to bring your dog in and out without explosions; it makes life easier for them and for the other animals and people in the waiting room. Also, if your dog can be brought in calmly, he's likely to be an easier patient than if he's spent twenty minutes in the waiting room panting and drooling and on a tight leash. Consider these options:

- ❖ If you have the first appointment of the day, you may find no one in the waiting room when you arrive.
- ❖ There may be a back entrance or a side hallway you can use.

- If other animals and/or people are in the waiting room, perhaps you and your dog can wait in an empty examining room—or even a storeroom.
- If you have a cell phone, perhaps you could wait in your car (if you have one) or around the corner, and the office could phone you when it's time to come in; a quick walk through a crowded waiting room with a fistful of treats is an improvement over those twenty minutes mentioned above.

FLEXIBILITY

Always remember to think outside the box—you don't have to be glued to walking in straight lines. We're so conditioned to "stay on the sidewalk" that sometimes it doesn't occur to us to duck between parked cars, to dash off the park path and up behind that first clump of bushes. You can swing wide around the blind corner or step off the curb if traffic permits. And, yes, calculated and careful jaywalking to escape an oncoming stimulus should become part of your repertoire. Every bit of the landscape that is not about to be occupied by a moving vehicle is available to you. Use it.

NEIGHBORS AND ADVISORS

You may have hostile neighbors or critics who just love to give you unsolicited and unwanted advice. While I can't give you advice that will work in every situation, some of these hints may be helpful to you.

A nice letter, explaining what you are doing and why and enlisting your neighbors' help (along with any one or more of the reinforcers listed below) may be useful. "It would help us so much if you could do X—we'd really like to make Freddy (as in Krueger) a better neighbor." Let them know that it won't be forever—just until your dog gets more comfortable. Perhaps you can call them as you are about to leave your dwelling. You can even tell them that they don't have to pick up the phone—just give you two minutes (or however long) after they hear your voice on the answering machine to make your exit; not having to answer will, of course, make it less tedious for them. If they have a dog and yours is dog–aggressive, find out that dog's potty schedule and go out at a different time.

Reinforcers to use for your neighbors: chocolate—Godiva if you can afford it—frequently; presents for their dog; a handwritten thank-you note; a single rose; a power tool; simple appreciation. You get the idea. Positively reinforce appropriate neighbor behavior, and it should increase. Changes for the better in your dog's behavior will be also be reinforcing for them.

WHEN YOU ARE BEING REASONABLE AND "THEY" ARE NOT

No matter where you live, every responsible dog owner runs into these kinds of situations—even with their "normal" dogs and even in the "boonies."

Scene One: You're walking your dog-aggressive dog in an area where dogs are supposed to be leashed. Someone with an off-leash dog approaches and refuses to leash her dog. When your dog barks and lunges, she says, "Boy, have you got a problem. Why don't you train your dog?"

Scene Two: You've spotted a great opportunity for a setup—a kid riding his bicycle up and down the sidewalk across the street, just below your dog's threshold for reactivity to children. You're feeding him the best treats in the world, and he is remaining calm and focused on you. You are feeling relaxed and pleased at your dog's positive response when a passerby says contemptuously, "You're bribing that dog."

Scene Three: The fellow down the block leaves his dog loose on the porch, even though this dog has attacked your reactive dog before. Despite your repeated pleas, he refuses to gate the porch or to keep his dog inside when he isn't there to supervise her.

Scene Four: You and your aggressive but well-managed dog are approaching an intersection that you can't avoid, but two people are standing right in the middle of the sidewalk, completely absorbed in their talk and not supervising the toddler who's starting to look interested in your dog. You politely ask them to keep their little girl at a distance because your dog is uncomfortable with children. They grudgingly move aside, but they also give you a dirty look and say, "You've got no business bringing that dog out in public."

It's safe to say that city and town dwellers encounter more inconsiderate and misguided people than country residents do simply because with a denser population you encounter more of every kind of personality. If you're a naturally even-tempered person, that's a great advantage.

But almost everyone loses their temper sometimes, and it can be especially hard to stay on an even keel if you're feeling defensive about your dog or if someone's carelessness or outright lawbreaking is undermining your careful work. Since shouting matches aren't going to do your dog any good or magically make rude people thoughtful of others, try not to be drawn into them, no matter how unfair the situation is.

It may be helpful to plan and rehearse responses to problem scenarios. Are there any you can use as training or counterconditioning opportunities? (For example, if you spot the loose dog soon enough, practice your escape maneuver.)

Sometimes more concrete action may be possible.

Scene One: Exact situations will vary, but if the other person's dog isn't coming after your lunging dog, then just walk the other way and get out of there. Drag your dog away if you have to. Now is the time for safety, not the time for training. This kind of person most likely will not leash her dog no matter what you say, so save your breath. If her dog is going after your dog, use some sort of pepper spray. This is not my favorite option, because, of course, I feel empathy for the loose attacking dog as well, but let's face it—you need to keep your dog (and yourself) safe.

Scene Two: Despite all of the brilliantly sarcastic comebacks you have instantly thought of, ignore them…just breathe in and breathe out. Repeat often.

Scene Three: Call Animal Control to deal with the neighbor who lets his dog run loose.

A group of people and a dog are blocking the sidewalk, so Kitt decided to take Georgie across the street to continue on her walk.

Scene Four: If you think there may be a problem, just go back the way you came, cross the street, or take a different route. Or you can simply say, "Excuse me, please. May I get by?" Wait for them to move, and then race your dog by (feeding the whole way) without giving any excuses about your dog. You are a person with a dog, they are blocking the sidewalk, and you have every right to ask them to move so you can get past. However, from their perspective, they may feel that they have a right to stand where they want to, so if they give you a hard time, just go in a different direction and let it go. If the child is still not under control, then by all means go to the other side of the street.

The key here is to remain calm and know—truly know—that being nasty to these types of people will never yield you a compliant response. Heck, some people fight even with police officers (and they have guns!), so thinking a rude person will listen respectfully to you may only get you into more trouble.

POTTY BREAKS

Dog-walk rush hour is often very predictable, which is a huge help to those of us with dog-aggressive dogs. Hot times are:

❖ The 6:30 to 9 A.M. slot.
❖ The lunchtime slot.
❖ The 3 P.M.-ish slot when people are picking up their kids from school and bring the dog along for the walk.
❖ 6 P.M., dinnertime.
❖ 10 P.M., bedtime.

When *not* to walk a dog-reactive dog: It's been pouring rain all weekend, and at 2 P.M. on Sunday the sun comes out. *Do not bring your dog reactive/aggressive dog out at 2:15!* It's the kind of "duh" moment we all have done just once, and I'd like to save you that experience.

Other witching hours are often around 5:30 A.M. and 11:30 P.M. when reactive dogs whose owners don't know what to do except try to avoid triggers come out. This may vary by locality, but in any given neighborhood many of the dogs are going to get their walks at more or less the same time on most days. Your job, of course, is to work around those time frames and as much as possible take your dog out when others are not.

RECAP

❖ *Practice the Big Three without your dog (positive mental imagery, finding your "safe place," and belly breathing).*
❖ *Start to make a mental note of where your dog's hot spots are.*
❖ *Enlist help from your neighbors.*
❖ *Think outside the box when looking for escape routes.*
❖ *If you can, get someone to help you by riding shotgun.*

Exercise in the Big City

START INDOORS

In the Big Book, I talked about training recalls—mostly off leash in safe areas or on a long line. If you don't have access to an outdoor space you can use safely, start this training indoors, doing the same exercises I described in Chapter Seven of the Big Book. Simon Says, Search and Rejoice, Run-Away Recall, and even End of the Rope Recall can all be trained indoors to start. Of course your distraction training will be harder in the Big City, but it can be done.

There are other recall games that you can play inside.

ROUND ROBIN PLUS

You will need at least two people for this. One person calls your dog and feeds with a huge jackpot of food and play (if your dog likes play) and then releases. Person Two then calls the dog and also jackpots with food and play. Repeat with everyone in your household. This is also a great way to physically exercise your dog, especially if you have a multiple-level dwelling. You can also add in collar grabs—the person calling the dog grabs the collar and jackpots. This will teach your dog that a collar grab means food is coming, so he isn't upset if you have to grab his collar when outside.

Practice collar grabs in many different contexts: when doing door etiquette, when out for a walk, when racing to a safety zone (practice at times when you don't actually *need* to escape into a safe place).

You should also practice saying your recall word in a panicked voice (this may not be much of a stretch for many of you). That way, when you should be breathing and talking calmly but instead are hyperventilating and screaming in terror, your dog will respond as if it were just another game.

One of my students has a human-aggressive dog that would get upset if his owner used a strong voice to ask people to keep their distance. I had her practice yelling at the TV in my building to "STAY AWAY!" while feeding her dog. A few days later, some teenagers moved to approach her dog although she had asked them politely to stop. Her dog remained completely calm as she screamed, "Sure, come closer, make my dog's day!" They promptly left.

WHISTLE TRAINING

Even if you never let your dog off leash, you need a recall for emergencies: leashes or collars can break, your grip may loosen when you're distracted, or the leash may be ripped out of your hand. I have become a real fan of whistle training, and I use the whistle as my really reliable recall signal (see Appendix 2 for Leslie Nelson's *Really Reliable Recall* DVD). We talk to and around our dogs all day long, and that verbal recall can get lost in the shuffle. If your dog is aroused (even in a state of pleasant excitement, not aggressive arousal), there's a good chance that he literally can't hear your voice. However, 99 percent of the time, the sound of the whistle will get through and the dog will respond instantly. Whistles are never angry, frustrated or upset; they remain neutral and sound the same every time. Plus, whistle training is very easy.

1. Week One: Every day, two to three times per day, spend a minute or two pairing the whistle with a treat. You don't need

a clicker—just whistle/treat as your dog sits in front of you. I prefer two short toots and one really long blast. If your dog gets out on a cold, windy, rainy, thunder-and-lightning night, the two short/one long blast will carry farther than one or two short toots. At this stage in the training, don't ask your dog to move—you're just teaching him that this new sound is very valuable and pays off every time.

You can get a whistle at any sporting goods store. Choose one with a long throat that you can hold in your teeth. Stay away from plastic whistles—the sound is too soft. A coach's whistle should work well for you.

2. Week Two: Play the Run-Away Recall game, but instead of using a verbal recall cue as your dog comes to you, do your two short/one long whistle blast and jackpot the heck out of him when he gets to you. Practice this every day, two to three times per day, for two to four minutes. Practice the same way with the Search and Rejoice game. You can also play the Round Robin game as listed above and give everyone in your household a whistle.

3. Week Three: At this point, you should be able to start using your whistle cue *before* the behavior takes place. Just hang around and watch your dog. If he gets slightly distracted or is in another room, but you can pretty much guarantee he will come if you call him, give the two short/one long blast and jackpot him when he gets to you. If he fails to come instantly more than two times, go back and practice the previous step again. Set up some easy distractions for your dog, gradually making them a little harder to ignore and always being sure that your reinforcers are better than what he is giving up. As you progress in whistle training, your dog will get better at coming away from harder distractions.

Practice your whistle training when you are out for a walk on a day pedestrian and dog traffic is light or when you find yourself with

Your whistle has the added benefit of being able to double as a call for help as you signal your dog, should you find yourself in a genuinely dangerous situation.

the golden opportunity of being in the country or an empty park with your dog on a long line. Let your dog sniff a little and then say his name softly. If he responds, give your whistle cue and jackpot him when he returns to you. Release him verbally to go sniff again and then, if he happens to look back at you, whistle. Or if you see his nose lift off the ground, whistle for him. Always jackpot him when he responds.

STAYS AND SELF-CONTROL

I am not a big fan of using a stay as part of a systematic desensitization session—especially in the beginning. I prefer to keep the dog busy. I look at stays this way: it is very stressful to remain completely still while scary bad things are around. Even though the dog can adjust his position, you are asking him to remain in the same spot—that is, he can't flee. If you have ever had an MRI, I am sure you can relate to this. It is incredibly hard to remain motionless while in that machine—the awful banging noise, knowing that if you have a muscle spasm the technician has to do the whole thing over, to say nothing of the fact that you may fear the test's result. Deep yoga breathing is not allowed (I tried that myself and was told "don't breathe so deeply"), and so your heart rate goes up and you may start to hyperventilate. These are not the makings of a positive association—and yet we know that nothing about the MRI is going to hurt us.

Now, having said all of that, I do understand that those of you living in a big city have to make stays a part of your foundation behaviors even during the early parts of your systematic desensitization program. You will need stays for door etiquette, and you can also train it in other contexts, as well. Many aggressive or reactive dogs lack self-restraint (for stays and other behaviors), but there are many games you can play to develop this much needed skill.

It is especially important for reactive dogs to learn to wait calmly while being leashed and not to charge out an open door. This is a matter of safety, of course, but also an important aspect of behavior modification with reactive/aggressive dogs. The dog that jumps around excitedly when you pick up the leash and then rushes through the doorway the instant you open the door is a dog that is aroused before you even start. Not a good situation.

The first time you begin work on door etiquette, plan for your exit to take a long time, depending on how much history your dog has of charging out the door. A good time to start teaching this exercise is *not* first thing on a weekday morning, when your dog's bladder is full and you need to get to work. Instead, pick an occasion when your dog has been well exercised, doesn't need to eliminate, and when you have enough time to stay calm and patient during the process. A bonus of living in an apartment building is that you can practice door etiquette at your apartment door, at the elevator or stairwell door, and again at the building door. It doesn't hurt, by the way, to practice sits and waits at the door when you're coming in, as well as when you're going out.

- Stay while dinner is being served—an easy one to do with the added benefit of teaching some self-control.
- Stay while a treat or toy is balanced on your dog's front paws (or for bonus points, while it is balanced on his nose).
- Stay while a toy is thrown.
- Stay while you hold a toy or treat off to one side and wait for eye contact before releasing the reinforcer.

When I train a stay, I rarely release the dog to go and get the object I dropped or threw. That will just reinforce the dog for the release, and you'll see your stays go down the tube. Go back to your dog to reinforce him and try not to let him get the object you dropped. (You can always reinforce him for the stay, tell him to stay again, and then go pick up the object you dropped.) Be creative and think up your own "stay" ideas.

Echo is doing "elevator etiquette."

REV UP AND COOL DOWN

This is a super game to help your dog rev up and cool down, continuing in our quest to teach your dog self-control and the ability to calm down quickly. The cool down part is the operative part here.

1. Move around for a few steps—slowly at first.
2. When your dog starts to get excited, walk very slowly and avoid eye contact.

I also teach "normal" dogs to do this. I just adopted a new Border Collie, Emma. In the beginning, if I revved her up even just a little, she would bite my arms and rip at my clothing. Because I've systematically played this game with her, she can now, after a few short months, keep her teeth to herself.

3. As soon as your dog slows down to match your pace, click and treat him. (I usually toss the treats on the ground.)
4. Repeat this a few times and then step up your "revving" to increase your dog's excitement.
5. Walk slowly again and when he slows down after being very aroused, make sure you reinforce him heavily for the calm behavior.

You can add in super fast downs—rev up, cool down, ask for a down, and then reinforce. You then have the option of playing with him again or going into a relaxing and calming session—perhaps a stay or a cuddle on the floor. Mix it up. This game also has the benefit of teaching your dog to switch gears—from arousal to calm in two seconds flat.

SCENT GAMES

The most basic scent game starts with telling your dog "find it!" Just toss some treats all over the floor and point to each treat as you say "find it." Once your dog gets the idea, you can start to say "find it" without using your finger to help him. After you've tossed a treat on the ground nearby a few times, you can start tossing some a bit farther away, so the dog has to hunt for it a little. Now it's time to start adding in degrees of difficulty.

- Cue your dog to stay, let him sniff the treat, and then hide the treat under a piece of paper in the dog's view. Reward the stay, then cue "find it!"
- While he stays, place the treat just out of his sight but uncovered.
- Place the treat out of his sight but this time cover it.
- While your dog watches, place the treat in an open paper bag.
- Put the treat in a bag while your dog is watching and put the bag down just out of sight.
- Go just out of sight and place the treat in the bag.
- Place the treat in a paper bag and twist the bag shut.
- Place the treat under a paper cup. Then try two, and then three paper cups: the dog gets the treat when he picks the correct cup. If he picks the wrong cup, try again.

You can see that the steps are geared toward making it easy for your dog to be successful. Once he gets into the game, make each step just a bit harder for him. Scent games are a great way to tire out your dog. If you are lucky enough to have a yard of any size whatsoever, feel free to feed your dog his dinner by scattering it all over and letting him "hunt" for his meals.

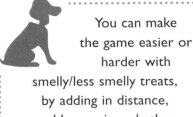

You can make the game easier or harder with smelly/less smelly treats, by adding in distance, and by varying whether the dog can see you hide the treat. It's not recommended that you hide the treat in the couch cushions!

Besides providing your dog with fun and mental exercise at home, "find it" can come in handy in sticky situations on the road. Can't avoid passing one of your dog's triggers? Start playing "find it" on the sidewalk as you walk and see if you can "Hansel and Gretel" your dog right past the problem. If you are lucky enough to have some grass handy, drop the treats in the grass to make it harder for your dog to find them, thus keeping his attention away from his scary bad things. This is very similar to the activity called "grazing" listed in the Big Book, except that you may be moving. If your dog enjoys the game enough and the trigger is far enough away, he may not even notice the trigger. If he does notice but continues to play the game, that's great! You've kept your dog under-threshold and you've also accomplished some counterconditioning.

Karen is playing "find it" while parallel walking with her dog's provoking stimuli. She is also using protected contact—in this case a chain-link fence.

FREE SHAPING

Free shaping (many people call it "capturing") is a great way to give your dog some mental exercise, teach him new skills such as problem solving, and help build his self-confidence. Free shaping also teaches you how to teach, correctly breaks down behaviors into tiny approximations, and does a great job in improving your timing. It doesn't matter what you free shape your dog to do—in fact, in the beginning, I recommend that you start with something simple and completely and utterly stupid, like doing a figure 8 around two chairs, crawling under a chair, nose targeting a piece of paper or spinning in a circle. Each of these behaviors can certainly be taught by luring the dog; however, that isn't the point of free shaping. The point is to have your dog figure out what you want by offering different types of behaviors and to teach you how to recognize those tiny, beginning steps.

Once your dog understands the concept of free shaping, the sky's the limit as to what you can free shape him to do. Some behaviors can be silly, some can be useful; it doesn't really matter. Here's the short list of what I have free shaped my dogs to do: flush the toilet, do competition heeling, close a door, perform on agility equipment, jump through hoops, ride a skateboard, swim, drag a wagon, put their toys away in a basket, bow, shake a paw, wave, spin in a circle, wipe their feet on a towel, grind their own nails on a doggie emery board (constructed from a piece of plywood and a sheet of sandpaper), roll over and cover themselves with a blanket, turn on the TV, and staple a piece of paper.

Lie Down on a Mat

Arm yourself with tons of treats and a clicker. Place a bathmat or dog bed on the floor and move a few feet away. If your dog looks at the mat/bed, click and toss a bunch of treats on it. You can click and treat as your dog continues to sniff the mat after eating the treats you already placed there. If he gets off it, just wait. To help him a little bit, you can look at him and then at the mat, look at him and then at the mat, and then stare at the mat. Each and every time he looks at the mat, click and toss a treat onto it. Pretty soon he should start to go to the mat instead of just looking at it. Click and treat each time he does so. After a minute or two, he should start to stay on the mat—click and jackpot. Then call him to you and see if he'll do it again. Once he is staying on the mat, you may "cheat" and ask him to lie down, and then click and jackpot. Call him off the mat again and repeat. Most dogs will start to go to the mat and lie down without prompting after about four to six repetitions. At this point you can name it "go to your mat" (or bed). Start to add in some more distance between you and the mat, so that eventually if your dog is annoying you and his mat is across the room, you can say, "Go to your mat," and he'll do it.

Wipe Your Feet

This game is not quite pure free shaping, but it is fun, very useful, and has many applications. Place a towel on the floor and while your dog is watching, put some very smelly treats underneath. (If your dog is more interested in toys than food, place a toy underneath the towel instead of treats.) Most dogs will sniff the towel trying to find the treats. If your dog doesn't, tap the towel with your finger and ask him to "find it." Click and treat for sniffing, dropping a treat on the towel. Continue to do this for a minute or so. Even if he is biting the towel, click and treat the first few times. You want him to be very interested in the towel. Then stop clicking and see if he will start to paw the towel in an attempt to get the treats. Any type of paw movement gets a click and treat. You should start to see your dog paw the towel more

Beau is wiping his feet on a towel.

Gus is nose targeting Gina's hand while in the presence of other people and dogs.

frequently and with more intensity. Once he is pawing it on a regular basis, you can name it "wipe your feet" as it is happening. Usually after another minute or two, you can start to say your cue a split second before he is about to paw the towel. To make this behavior of "pawing" even more useful, get a piece of plywood and glue the coarsest sandpaper you can find onto it. Place it on the floor and ask your dog to "wipe your feet." Voila! Instant nail grinding! This is especially useful if you have a dog that will not allow his feet to be touched.

Nose Targeting and More

Start this behavior by having a treat and your clicker in one hand. Hold out your empty hand. You dog will either sniff it or touch it with his nose. Click and treat. Repeat about a dozen times and then name it "touch" as your dog is touching your hand. You will use this to get your dog to look away from his provoking stimuli when you are out and about.

To turn this behavior into a fun game, take a piece of paper and hold it out in the same manner (you don't have to say anything). Click and treat him for touching it with his nose. Do a few more repetitions and once he is nosing it on a regular basis, tape the paper to a door at nose level. Click and treat him any time he comes anywhere near the paper and be sure to offer the treat at the paper. As he becomes more proficient, open the door slightly. Then click and treat him for moving the door. Repeat a bunch of times and then hold out until he pushes the door hard enough to close it. Some dogs may end up using their feet to close the door.

During a training session or walk, you can use repeated targeting to your hand to walk your dog past triggers. The idea is to have him practice an enjoyable learned behavior under a little bit of stress, as well as to keep him focused on you.

STAYING MOTIVATED

What helped me to stay motivated with Shadow during the long and sometimes frustrating training process was to teach him very difficult behaviors. Drop on recall, scent discrimination, go-outs, directed jumping, moving stand, and retrieve on the flat and over a jump were only a few of the things I worked on with him. Even if I never was going to actually compete (which I now do), the process made me a better trainer and added a new dimension to our relationship—the behaviors were challenging and fun to train, and we both came to appreciate each other more fully.

NO TIME TO TRAIN

If you find that you are too busy on any given day (especially rainy ones) to give your dog enough mental and physical exercise, by all means, bring out the frozen stuffed Kongs or raw beef marrow bones for recreational chewing enjoyment. My own dogs act like they have been drugged after a bout of chewing.

You can also wrap up a toy in a towel (if your dog likes toys) and ask your dog to find it. He then has to puzzle out how to get the toy out of the towel. Start easy by only placing the towel over the toy; then add in one fold, then two, and finally get really evil in how you wrap up the toy. I use this game when I am in a hotel room with my three dogs and there is no room to do anything.

My dog Beau made up this next game, and I call it "Skee Ball." You are on the bed. Your dog is on the floor. You roll the ball along the bed and try to get it past your dog. You get a point if you get it past your dog, and he gets a point if he stops it. You can also play this game with both of you on the floor.

RELAXING

While outdoor aerobic exercise is helpful when you can get it, mental exercise is just as important when you have a vigorous dog whose issues make it impossible to just head on over to the dog park and let 'er rip. Mental exercise can spell the difference between sanity and nuttiness for both dog and person. Because many of the indoor games are training in disguise, they increase the dog's general responsiveness and confidence.

Exercise doesn't always have to be racing and running—in fact, if you do too much of this, it can actually overstress your dog. You want a nice mix of mental stimulation, some aerobic exercise, and some opportunities to just be a dog (as in a long, slow, sniffy, on-lead outdoor walk). You might want to add in some TTouch (see Appendix 2) and some stretching exercises. There's even a book/video on meditating with your dog (again, see Appendix 2).

Perhaps your local park is big enough to include areas that aren't often frequented by other people or dogs, or maybe both you and your dog enjoy getting out on a rainy or snowy day when most of the world only wants to stay home and snooze on the couch. If you don't have a typical nine-to-five schedule, you may be able to take your dog many places during off hours when you're not likely to encounter provoking stimuli—or at least when the problems are few and far enough between that you can see them coming and take evasive action. Do some research; for many or most dogs—even aggressive ones—and in many or most cities, there will be places and times where you can enjoy a fairly stress-free stroll together.

The experience will be good for you as well as your dog. One of the most dispiriting and disheartening aspects of having an aggressive dog is that you can't freely do many of the things people with "normal" dogs enjoy without ever thinking twice. That quiet park path where hardly anybody else seems to go is an opportunity to have a more relaxed and normal relationship with your dog. Places like it exist almost everywhere. Find them, use them, enjoy them.

RECAP

- Practice the many recall games listed in the Big Book and in this one. There is no such thing as "too good a recall."
- Practice stays and make them a daily part of your life.
- Playing the rev up and cool down game is a great way to teach your dog to switch gears at the drop of a hat.
- Be sure to add in tons of mental stimulation and free shaping to your dog's life.

Prevention

CHANGING THE MEANING OF SIGNALS

Human anxiety signals—shortness of breath or no breath at all, hyperventilation, a panicked voice, screaming if you don't normally scream, tightening up on the leash, or freezing in position—are produced by all of us at times. Since we (unfortunately) communicate our tension to our dogs, it's useful to teach your dog that all these signs of anxiety are nothing to worry about—they simply mean "cookies are coming."

This is a matter of pairing each of your own personal anxiety signals with food. Please be sure to practice this when you're not actually in a panic. For instance, you can gently tug on the leash and immediately give your dog a treat. *(This is not to be confused with a leash correction.)* This teaches your dog that tightening up on the leash signals that good things are about to happen. Repeat this hundreds—if not thousands—of times. If your dog hits the end of the leash on his own, the tightening up thus can actually become a cue for him to be calm.

You can practice sternly telling or even shouting at someone (a friend or inanimate object) to stay away and give your dog a jackpot each time. If you are really good at visualization, practice hyperventilating or holding your breath and grabbing the collar in a death grip while feeding your dog. Train for whatever you normally do when panicked so that the behavior becomes no big deal for your dog.

Just as you can teach your dog to remain calm in response to your panic signals, you can and should do the same with other noises. Dogs barking, skateboards, elevators dinging, garbage trucks—you can train a positive association to whatever noises your dog alerts to. The more you can reduce the number of stimuli that upset your dog, the lower his general level of arousal will be. This will make it easier to keep him below threshold in many of those situations that you can't control.

When Shadow needed to be measured for his agility height card, I diligently practiced not only the actual measuring with strangers but also holding his collar very tightly. When the big day came, I was a basket case, holding his collar so tightly it was a wonder he could breathe. My stress signals went through the roof when the judge, whom I'd warned about Shadow being nervous around strangers, put her face right in his! But because I had practiced so much, Shadow stayed relaxed and looked at me with an expression that clearly said, "Mom, what is *your* problem?"

Some people have success with sound desensitization CDs, but I've found that while some dogs can learn to be calm when listening to the CD, their response to the actual item itself doesn't change. Plus, some dogs never seem to register hearing the sounds on the CD at all. However, if you can find a CD that's a close fit with the kinds of sounds that arouse your dog, by all means try it. You can also make your own recording from the sounds in your neighborhood.

As you already know, the difficulty with desensitization done "live" is that you generally can't work systematically because you can't predict when the noise or sight will appear or how intense it will be. There are always exceptions—if the dog down the block reliably races to his front window and barks frantically at your dog as you walk by, then you can learn to be prepared for that particular situation.

When you can't predict the occurrence of the scary bad thing, the trick is to stay prepared and alert. Prepared means that you always keep treats ready, and alert means that your own awareness of these sounds must be heightened, so they become a cue to you to feed your dog instantly. The idea is that when you hear the sound or see the sight, you instantly, automatically, and without thinking give your dog treat after treat after treat. (The process should be as automatic as driving. Once you are comfortable driving, you rarely have to actually think of what to do when you see a red traffic light: you simply stop.)

This next series of photos is a perfect example of thinking fast. I was in a town taking pictures for this book when all of a sudden a waitress came rushing out of a restaurant ("Oh! Is that a Border Collie? I love Border Collies!").

The waitress is coming down the steps. I quickly call Shadow to come...

We continue to move backward toward the bench (our safety net). Photos by Gina Boderck.

The waitress is still moving toward me, so I continue to move backward.

I am now on the opposite side of the bench, talking to the waitress with my back to her, still feeding Shadow. Photos by Gina Boderck.

As with driving, being cognizant of the sights and sounds around you and reacting immediately and appropriately simply takes practice. As you become better at it, your own stress will lessen, which in turn will lead your dog to become calmer. An added benefit is that the more aware you are of your environment, the less it will be able to take you by surprise.

DOORBELL AND ELEVATOR CUES

As you can see, I am a big fan of taking a previously scary stimulus and making it mean something else. For instance, with dogs that go ballistic at the sound of the doorbell, you can simply teach them that the ring now means "go to your crate." If you live in an apartment or condo, and your dog gets aroused at the sound of the elevator ding (because it predicts the entry of more passengers or the arrival of strangers at your home), you can turn the sound into a cue for the dog to get between your legs.

Doorbell Ring
Arm yourself with tons of treats and a willing friend.
1. Have your friend ring the doorbell.
2. Call your dog to you and run with him to the crate saying your "kennel up" cue word.
3. Give him wads of treats for getting in the crate. Release him from the crate and do it again—the doorbell rings, you and your dog race to see who can get to the crate faster, you give tons of treats in the crate.
4. Repeat this about ten times.

Usually by this time, your dog is starting to figure out that the cue is the doorbell, the behavior is "get in my crate," and the consequence is that he gets wads of treats.

In a different session, repeat the above steps to review, and then on the second rep, just stand there once the doorbell rings and wait. Let's see if the dog can figure this out by himself, without you running to the crate with him. Wait for at least fifteen seconds. If your dog doesn't run to the crate, help him a little by whispering "go kennel." Then once he is in the crate, give him wads of treats. Repeat again and help him as little as possible. Do about five or six more reps, continuing to have a party each time he gets in his crate. Most dogs will "get it" by this time, but if yours doesn't, don't worry—just keep trying.

Now you want to increase the time he is in his crate before you give him treats, since you really don't want to have to run to the crate (depending on where in the house the crate is in relation to the door) each time the doorbell rings. Your bell ringer rings the bell, the dog goes to his crate, and you walk slowly to the crate while he waits patiently for the party. Keep doing this, gradually increasing the time your dog stays in his crate before you feed him.

Now it's time to add live people into the mix. Start this with one person, not fifty. Your friend rings the bell, the dog goes to his crate, you let the person in the house and have him or her sit quietly while you race to the crate and have a party with your dog. Then you bring the dog out of the crate (on leash if needed at first) and heavily reinforce him for paying attention to you. Repeat many times.

Once he is completely calm with the above steps, you may allow your dog to greet your guest (if he isn't human–aggressive). If he is wild and frenzied, say nothing, do nothing (other than hang on tightly to his leash, being sure not to yank back), and wait for him to chill out. Reinforce for the calm behavior and try again in a few minutes— do not let him greet your guest at this point. Repeat the process again until he can remain calm at all times, from the ringing of the doorbell, to him racing to his crate, to you allowing your guest in the house, to you having a party in the crate, to you putting the leash on him and bringing him into the room where your friend is.

Once your dog remains calm with each of these steps, you can gradually add one new person at a time. If at any time the dog becomes frenzied, just ask him to "go kennel" and start over. It is important to use friends who will not pet or talk to him if he is being silly. It is also important that you don't pet or talk to him either; just coolly and dispassionately take him back to his crate and try again later.

Depending on your specific situation, you may not be able to allow your dog to greet your guest. But if you can get to the point where the dog is at least comfortable being in the same room, you will have made some major progress.

Elevator *Ding!*

As with most behaviors, this one is pretty easy to train. Start training it at home.

1. Have your dog in heel position.
2. Lure him to back up and come between your legs and sit (that way you can get a good grip on his collar or harness for additional safety).
3. Click and treat.
4. Repeat dozens of times and then start to name the behavior ("peek" works well).
5. Start to fade your hand lure.

Gina is luring Gus to back up...

...and then luring him in between her legs.

Once your dog is good at this new behavior, bring him out into the hallway where the elevator is. So you can have greater control of the situation and get more reps in, have a friend go up and down in the elevator so it *dings* more often. That way you also know no one will actually be getting off the elevator. As you hear the *ding*, give your cue word and heavily reinforce your dog when he gets between your legs. Repeat as many times as you can without driving your neighbors crazy. Once your dog is comfortable doing the behavior in the presence of the *ding*, start to fade your verbal cue to see whether he has made the association of *ding* equals "peek." You most certainly can continue to use a verbal cue and/or hand signal, but it is also fun to see if you can teach your dog to do the behavior with *ding* as the cue.

BREAKING IT DOWN

Just as when you teach a behavior you break it down into small approximations, so, too, can you break down your dog's provoking stimuli. For example, suppose your dog freaks out at kids on skateboards. You have the noise, the sudden approach, the speed and the body position of the kid, including what he or she is doing with their arms and legs. If you can desensitize your dog to even just a few of these "pieces," it may help your dog react less strongly to the whole package.

Look and listen for skateboards. If you see/hear one, you can be sure your dog sees/hears it, too. At any faint sound of a skateboard, shovel the treats. This is also a situation you can work on at home. Borrow or purchase a skateboard. Have someone move the skateboard around very slowly at a distance. As soon as the skateboard begins to move and your dog looks at it, shovel treats. When the skateboard stops, stop shoveling treats. As your dog develops a positive association with the slowly moving skateboard, your assistant can move it faster and faster, with you shoveling treats all the while. Continue in the same manner and gradually add in the other elements—rapid movement toward the dog (as if to pass, not run over) and then rapid movement toward the dog with unusual arm gestures.

When considering any scary thing that is a problem for your dog, give some thought to what its component parts are, where and when these parts might appear at a low enough intensity that they don't upset your dog, and which parts you might be able to replicate and work on systematically. By breaking these triggers down and practicing in your living room, yard, or other safe place, you can (with many dogs and many stimuli) make good progress simply counterconditioning and desensitizing on the fly. As you continue the process, you're likely to find that the real, unpredictable things don't push your dog over threshold as fast or with as much intensity as they used to. As a result, your dog's overall arousal and stress levels will drop. And arousal and stress, of course, are big contributors to aggressive behavior.

If you have the room to do so, make sure you are asking for some fun behaviors during these types of sessions. Movement and focus on a different task will help relax both of you and will help increase your focus on each other. When at all possible, avoid the static stay.

WHERE'S THE DOG?

I have had great success using this behavior with dog-aggressive dogs. I must point out, however, that I don't use it with "raw" dogs—those that as of yet, have no training, no name recognition, no recall, and no connection with their owners or that don't know that *click* means *treat*. You must have these basics down before you start to teach this behavior.

Very simply, when your dog sees another dog say, "Where's the dog?" in a happy, excited voice and then *before* your dog reacts, click and treat. The first few times it may be very hard to click before he pops off, so this will be a good exercise in timing for you. In the beginning, you can also add in your come cue: "Where's the dog? Come!" If you can, practice when the distance is great to minimize the intensity of your dog's potential reaction.

Once both you and your dog are good at this, you can start to say this new cue before your dog actually spots the other dog. What may very well happen is that your dog will scan the environment, zero in on the dog, and instantly look back to you.

GET OUT OF DODGE

If you have a reactive/aggressive dog in the Big City, you'll be relying heavily on your escape cue. The best case is that while *you* know you're getting out of Dodge, your dog only knows that all of a sudden

Jane is practicing "getting out of Dodge" with Ruby and is using the tree as her escape route.

Here, Jane is practicing "getting out of Dodge" with Ruby by scooting into a doorway.

you're both making tracks in a new direction *and that he's having a blast doing so.* In other words, ideally your escape cue should not predict for your dog the presence of any of his triggers. In the real world, he may well learn the wrong association (as in "scary thing coming") despite your best efforts. For instance, if he is highly reactive toward other dogs, and on your last walk of the evening you have the bad luck to encounter half a dozen dogs and need to use your escape cue each time, the odds are pretty good that the next time you practice the escape cue without any dogs around, he is going to look around for a dog.

If you teach the escape cue as a fun and happy game and practice it regularly in the absence of triggers (or in situations where the scary thing is present but not intense enough to go over your dog's threshold), it should lessen any bad reaction from your dog. The escape is wonderfully easy to teach.

1. Pick a verbal cue. It should be something that will fly out of your mouth easily when a trigger appears, and should carry no hint of emergency. "Let's go this way!" "Sayonara!" "Bye-bye!" "Are you READY!?" Silly is good.
2. Have some good treats ready.
3. Say your escape cue in a happy voice and run in a different direction. Be sure the leash remains loose; that is, you don't want to be popping your dog's collar. Give your dog tons of treats for staying with you.

Practice moving in different directions, not just making U turns, and refrain (if you can, of course!) from using the escape in actual sticky situations until you've put in quite a few repetitions and your dog is always responding appropriately. Even when your dog is doing this happily and instantly, please reinforce each and every time.

Once you start using the escape in real situations, continue to practice it even when no scary stuff is around. That way you will help assure that your dog won't react or scan the environment in

I suspect, though I can't prove, that the escape cue can have an important beneficial side effect. Sometimes aggressive displays occur because flight is unavailable (for example, the dog is on leash), and an animal's only options are fight or freeze. After many successful escapes from upsetting situations, some dogs learn that we will help them leave and they therefore experience a lower level of distress—which in turn makes the "fight" reaction less likely.

This small area has many escape routes—Kitt and Georgie are between two bushes, Karen and Jerome are on the left side of the pole, and Jane and Ruby are between a bush and the bench.

the absence of triggers. If you encounter a series of situations that aren't interspersed with plenty of "triggerless" escape practice, your dog is quite likely to stay with you if you have practiced enough. If the day has been a really bad one, and everyone in the world seems to be out to get you and your dog, by all means pack up and go home. Try again later or the next day.

RECAP

- ❖ Make your panic signals a cue to your dog that cookies are coming.
- ❖ Be prepared—the instant you see or hear your dog's triggers, you instantly hand out treats.
- ❖ Learn to break down each aggressive incident/trigger, so you can replicate it in tiny steps in order to desensitize your dog to each one.
- ❖ If your dog is dog–aggressive, play the Where's the Dog? game.
- ❖ Practice your "get out of Dodge" cue even when you don't need it.

Heeling and Loose-Leash Walking in the Big City

MUZZLES: PROS AND CONS

Before I get to loose-leash walking your aggressive dog, the possibility of using (or not using) a muzzle needs to be addressed. The obvious advantage of having your dog wear a muzzle is that while he's wearing it, he can't bite. If your dog has a history of biting in certain scenarios (or you think he may bite) and you can't avoid those situations—for example, going to the vet—then there aren't really any further questions to ask in this case. (Even though Shadow really likes our vet, I do still muzzle him because that way I remain completely calm and so does he. Because I live in the boonies, that is the only time he is muzzled.) Also, people tend to keep their distance from muzzled dogs, and that can help keep your dog below threshold. Finally, the knowledge that your dog can't inflict a bite may help keep you calm, especially when blindsided.

Believe it or not, there are people who, upon seeing a muzzled dog, still race up to him, arms outstretched, wanting to pet him, even after you ask them to stay away. It happened to me at a vet clinic with a vet tech reaching out for Shadow. I made sure that I told the vet so as to avoid a disaster in the future with someone else's dog.

If you think it may help, have the dog wear a pretty bandanna, ribbon, or bow. It sends a different message and, if you're lucky, will distract some people from noticing the muzzle at all.

On the other hand, if they're racing up to see your dog, the neckwear is probably *too* cute.

Muzzling also has a couple of practical disadvantages: it can be hard to feed treats through the side of a basket muzzle, whereas a dog can still bite someone through an open-front nylon muzzle. (I was a groomer—I know.)

It is also important to consider possible psychological and behavioral disadvantages. Muzzles are conspicuous. To the public at large they scream, "Aggressive dog!", and sometimes the reaction is to gasp, jump back, point, stare, and grab children by the arms and drag them away, while giving the owner of the dog dirty looks. This goes double if your dog is large or belongs to a breed with a reputation for aggression. It would be a good bet that even when passersby aren't visibly tense, their pupils dilate, and their body language shows some subtle unease.

You can see where this is going. Just as a dog-reactive dog is more likely to feel tense in the presence of another reactive dog than in the presence of a calm dog with soft body language that's sniffing the ground and not paying him any mind, a dog that's reactive to humans will feel more uneasy when people stare, gasp, or otherwise manifest unease. Even dogs that generally are comfortable and relaxed with people may become more watchful of humans who act "weird" in this way.

By making you and your dog conspicuous, a muzzle may actually increase your stress. It's not much fun to hear the word "vicious" come out of strangers' mouths as you walk your dog. Depending on your dog's history, muzzling him in public may be the most responsible thing you do. But if so, bear in mind the possible fallout, and consider investing time in desensitizing your dog to such human responses as staring, gasping, and sudden backward movement. While you're at it, cultivate a thick skin to limit the wear and tear on your own psyche.

If you decide that using a muzzle is the best thing at this point for you and your dog, be sure to acclimate your dog to it—please *don't* just shove it on and go for a walk. It is actually quite easy to train a dog to accept a muzzle and takes only about fifteen minutes or so. Grab some peanut butter, treats, and a clicker.

1. Place a wad of peanut butter in the muzzle. Hold the muzzle out to your dog and let him lick off the peanut butter.
2. Repeat the above step a few times.
3. Put less peanut butter in this time and when your dog is just about done licking, click and place the treat through the side of the muzzle. This takes a bit of coordination on your part. If it is too much, use your click word "yes" instead of the clicker.
4. Repeat the above steps a few times, gradually putting in less and less peanut butter and doing more clicking and treating through the side of the muzzle.
5. Now just hold out the muzzle without peanut butter and wait. If he looks at the muzzle or puts his head in to see if he missed a bit, click and treat through the side of the muzzle. If you can, do some rapid-fire treating to encourage him to keep his head in the muzzle (without forcing him—you want it to be all his idea).
6. Repeat the above step until your dog is happily placing his face in the muzzle and holding it there. Then you can strap on the muzzle, all the while clicking and treating.
7. Play with him with the muzzle on—not with toys of course, but you can race around and get him to chase you and click and treat him for staying with you. Practice your sits, downs, and stays with the muzzle on as well.

TRAINING TIPS

In Chapter Seven of the Big Book, I talk about the whys and hows of training attention heeling. In the city, you can start to teach attention heeling in basically the same manner, although your dog will be on a

Shadow is eating peanut butter in a muzzle.

Shadow placing his face in the muzzle without the use of peanut butter. Photos by Gina Boderck.

short leash. Depending on your dog's history of pulling, you may have to start the training in your house or apartment. Keep these tips in mind:

Walk your dog hungry. Feel free to feed your dog only on leash walks and during other training. There is no law that I know of that says your dog must be fed in a bowl. Heck, there is nothing wrong with him working for a living—you do! To keep this fairly simple, use very high value treats and toys during all training, not just loose-leash walking—don't plan on getting great results with boring reinforcements. Remember, the more interesting you are, the more your dog will focus on you.

Schedule training walks carefully. Difficulty rises along with the dog's general excitement level, degree of fatigue, and bladder and bowel fullness. As a rule, the most difficult time to achieve any semblance of a loose-leash walk will be the first walk of the morning, when the dog is well-rested, eager, and dying for a pee and poop. The better rested you are, the higher the quality of your food reinforcers (and other reinforcers, too), and the more mentally prepared you are to be calm and patient, the more success you'll have.

Exercise before you walk. Use indoor games and mental exercise to take the edge off your dog's energy and build his focus on you. Obviously this isn't possible before the first potty walk of the day, so be flexible. Notice and reinforce calm behavior throughout the day.

Train your pre-walk behaviors. Practice your walk preparations. Your dog should sit calmly when you leash him and assemble your own gear and while you open the door. It is very important that he isn't super-charged even before he leaves the gate. As mentioned in Chapter Three, be sure your door etiquette behaviors are up to snuff.

Consider your equipment. First of all, don't worry about using a clicker to mark the behavior of loose-leash walking unless you are very skilled at scanning your environment at all times, holding the leash and clicker, and reacting instantly when scary things loom out of nowhere. Use a verbal marker, such as "yes!" instead. I myself find sometimes that using the clicker is too cumbersome—too many things to hold. Be sure to prime your "yes!" beforehand so that it has become as strong a marker signal to your dog as the click.

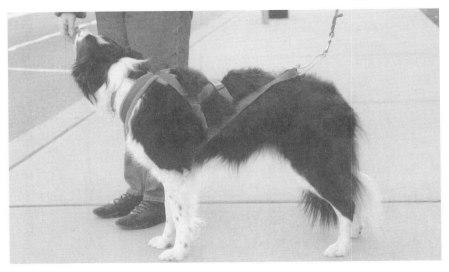

Shadow with his X-back sledding harness on—note how it hooks back by his tail.

Shadow with his leather tracking harness. Photos by Gina Boderck.

I have a grip on Shadow's harness and am feeding him while people are walking by. Photo by Gina Boderck.

I am a big fan of using certain types of harnesses: the X-back sledding harness for dogs under forty pounds and a leather tracking harness for dogs over that weight (see Appendix 2). I like these two types of harnesses for two main reasons: (1) they are very comfortable for the dog, and if he does hit the end of the leash, it doesn't hurt him, so he will not experience any further bad associations; (2) the pressure is spread out, keeping the opposition reflex to a minimum, and thus the dog pulls much less. An added benefit to either one of these harnesses is that the straps are large enough to just grab and hold on to, which will give you better leverage and strength if a real emergency happens.

I am not a big fan of front hook harnesses for several reasons. Although I like them in theory, they don't really fit properly—if the dog pulls, the straps dig into his chest or armpits, causing discomfort. I simply haven't seen dogs relax in front hook harnesses the way I have seen them do in the other harnesses. But if your dog loves his front hook harness, then by all means continue to use it.

The same holds for any type of head halter. Head halters present a few additional problems: (1) they restrict the dog's ability to give appropriate calming signals; (2) by forcing your dog's head away from something, they place him in a vulnerable position—his hind end is now facing the scary thing and he may feel that he can't protect himself, which will do nothing to help his frame of mind; and (3) if the dog does lunge/aggress, the risk for a whiplash injury may be high. I do understand that in the Big City you may have no other choice. Perhaps your dog outweighs you, and you can't possibly control him in any other way for now. "For now" is the operative phrase here. With this type of training aid, the dog needs to be gradually accustomed to it, and as soon as possible weaned off it.

You may find it useful to use two different kinds of harnesses— one for "potty walks, we are not training now," and a different one for "we are training now." When training my own dogs, I don't switch harnesses but instead use a different word. I will teach you how to do that in a minute.

THE MECHANICS

You can take the exercises in the Big Book and start to train loose-leash walking in your house, yard, or other safe place. Once you begin to teach loose-leash walking, every single walk will have to be a training walk (unless you switch equipment or word, as mentioned above).

Because you will be doing most of your training on a six-foot leash, you'll have to be a bit more "rigid" than your country cousins may have to be. Pick one side for your dog to be on. I prefer the left side even though I am right-handed, mostly because that is what I am used to; plus, it leaves my stronger side free in case I need it.

There are two kinds of loose-leash walking:

- Loose-leash walking where your dog can be anywhere near you, sniffing and enjoying the weather as long as the leash is loose.

Shadow is loose-leash walking. Note my left arm position—it is down and swinging, and while he is not in heel position, he isn't pulling either.

Now Shadow is heeling. Note my left arm position—it is up at my waist. I am also holding the leash in my right hand, so I can feed out of my left hand. His attention is riveted on me. Photos by Gina Boderck.

❖ Attention heeling where your dog will be in perfect heel position, looking adoringly up at your face.

I like to train attention heeling first because you will need your dog to focus on you many times during your day to keep him out of trouble. We all know this scene: You are minding your own business and your dog is loose-leash walking when all of a sudden a trigger pops up. By teaching your dog a specific heel cue, you will be able to get his attention back to you instantly and heel past the scary bad thing without incident.

ATTENTION HEELING

For the green dog or the one that has a history of pulling, you will play the "feint left, feint right" game before moving on to the next step. This works just as it sounds: you will feint left and feint right, clicking and treating your dog for following you. Move in all different directions and make it fun for him to stay with you. You can "stalk" him and then race around, move fast, move slow, and reinforce him for being glued to you. Once he is good at that, proceed with the next step. Even if your dog already has good solid focus on you, play this game anyway—it will make being with you more fun.

Practice backups from the Big Book. Once your dog is staying with you on a consistent basis, pivot (you turn to your right) so that your dog is on the left in heel position. Put your left arm up at your waist (this will become your hand signal), click, and then treat with your left hand (clicker and leash are in your right hand), using a high rate of reinforcement as your dog stays in heel position. Be sure that your left arm goes back up to your waist after each treat. Then you can further discriminate by clicking and treating only when your dog is not only in heel position, but is also looking up at your face. I am asking you to have your leash in your right hand for a reason—if you feed with your right hand, your dog may continually walk in front of you to get to the treat faster. You thus have a good chance of him tripping you—not pretty.

As your dog gets better at remaining in heel position, you can start to name this behavior. Common words are "heel" or "strut." Choose a word that you will remember and start to name the behavior as your dog is looking up at you. It will look like this: you are moving, your dog is in heel position, your arm is up at your waist, he looks up at your face, and you say "heel" and then click and treat.

In the beginning, you will give a high rate of reinforcement (for instance, click and treat just about every step) and use your heel word a second or two before you click and treat. As your dog gets better at attention heeling, you can begin to lengthen the time between clicks and also vary the reinforcement type so you aren't using food 100 percent of the time.

If you practice at home first or in a relatively boring and trigger-free area, you can even get this behavior with a green dog, a dog that has a long history of pulling, or a highly energetic dog. Again, it may help to use different equipment for training walks and walks during which you simply have to get from point A to point B.

LOOSE-LEASH WALKING

Now that your dog is doing attention heeling, you can teach him to walk on a loose leash. Pick a place and a time when you can pretty much assume there won't be any triggers. Let your dog sniff around for a bit and when you think he will respond, say his name. If he looks at you, click and treat and keep walking, perhaps in a different direction (keep the leash loose!). The first time he complies and walks with you without pulling, be sure to heavily reinforce him with plenty of food, petting, and praise. Walk for a minute or two more, say his name again and if he responds, click and treat and keep walking. He should start to stick around closer to you. Once he is good at not pulling, you can name this behavior with your loose-leash walking cue, "let's go," "with me," or whatever word you want to use. Be sure to put your left arm down by your side for loose-leash walking, as this will also become a cue to him that he doesn't have to be in heel position.

CHANGE OF DIRECTION CUE

I find a change of direction cue very useful in many situations. I feel it is just polite behavior on your part to let your dog know that you are changing direction. It is very simple to train. As you are about to change direction, say your dog's name and "this way" in a happy voice and click and treat him for following you. This is basically the same thing as your escape cue.

TROUBLESHOOTING

I know that loose-leash walking is harder to train for some dogs than for others. If you've been practicing loose-leash walking conscientiously for several sessions, and you're not seeing substantial improvement, see the list below and decide of any of these things could be the problem:

> ❖ Have you done enough prep work in the basics as outlined above?

This owner is addicted to a tight leash. Note that the dog isn't pulling, but the owner is.

❖ Are you watching your timing? If your dog pulls, and you stand still (commonly called "be a tree") and wait for him to come back to you, are you clicking and treating right away? Does he then take the treat and go right back to pulling? If so, you may be creating a behavior chain "pull ahead, stop, come back, get a treat, pull ahead…." The better option is to wait for him to come back, say, "Nice of you to show up," take a few steps of heeling in a different direction, and then click and treat.

❖ Watch your rate of reinforcement—are you too cheap with the treats?

❖ Are your treats better than the smell of squirrels?

❖ Are you too boring with how you reinforce, and are you using the same old one treat at each and every click?

❖ Are you losing focus on your dog?

❖ Are you giving your dog enough time to just be a dog and sniff to his heart's content? Be sure to verbally release him frequently to give him some time to relax. No one of us should be expected to "work" all of the time.

Are you addicted to a tight leash? I see this all of the time—owners trying to teach their dogs to walk on a loose leash and yet they not only have a death grip on the leash, they also have it pulled so tight that the dog is choking—even when their dogs aren't pulling. Try to be more aware of what you are doing, not just what your dog is doing. One of my favorite analogies is from horseback riding (if you have ever ridden dressage, just think "subtle"): if you are constantly pulling on the reins, the horse will constantly fight with you. If you are easy on his mouth and handle the reins with a very soft and light touch, he will respond much better to what you are asking him to do.

RECAP

❖ Decide whether a muzzle would be helpful or harmful in your particular situation.

❖ If you decide it would be helpful, train your dog to accept the muzzle before you need to use it.

❖ Don't skip the basics of training loose-leash walking.

❖ Make loose-leash walking fun for your dog, and be sure to use reinforcers other than just food.

❖ Be sure to train a loose-leash walking cue, as well as a heeling cue.

❖ Try not to get discouraged.

❖ Change to one of the harnesses listed in Appendix 2.

Too Late for Prevention

DAMAGE CONTROL I: WHEN YOU CAN'T ESCAPE AND YOUR DOG GOES OVER-THRESHOLD

Scene One: Your dog reacts explosively to the sight of oncoming Labrador Retrievers (oh—that wiggly body language!). The traffic is against you, so you can't escape across the street and here comes the wiggliest Lab you've ever seen, (on a flexi leash no less!), and his owner is completely oblivious and talking on a cell phone. There you are, stuck on the sidewalk, with absolutely nowhere to go.

Scene Two: Your dog lunges and snarls at UPS drivers (oh—that brown uniform and noisy truck!). You're enjoying your morning walk on a quiet day when the new UPS driver on the local route pulls over next to you and hops out of the van to ask about an address he can't find.

Crises like these pretty much divide themselves into two types: the kind where you can see the train coming but are tied to the tracks, and the kind where the train pops out of nowhere with no warning.

In Scene One, you actually do have some time to prepare. Keep your voice and demeanor calm, breathe and create as much distance as you can manage between you and the scary thing. Make sure you have a good grip on your dog's leash or collar if you need to (or hold on to the straps of his harness—see Chapter Four). Because you have already practiced this, he should remain pretty calm.

55

The next step is to feed your dog. Keep the treats coming as quickly as you can, being sure to maintain a calm, steady demeanor. Depending on the exact situation, you can even scatter food on the ground (grazing—see Chapter Nine in the Big Book) to keep your dog's focus elsewhere. Speak to your dog slowly and softly and if you are having difficulty breathing, then sing. Personally, I sing "Happy Birthday" because that is the only song I can reliably remember the words to when I am freaked out. If you are singing, you are breathing. The fact that you are singing "Happy Birthday" in a public place for no reason discernable to the surrounding populace may make you laugh out loud and relax both you and your dog.

Scene Two: The train popped out of nowhere and you are loosely tied to the tracks. When confronted with that kind of situation, you will utilize a few behaviors all in a split second: for your dog, come front and stay; for you, grab the collar/harness, keep one eye on your dog and one eye on the person, sing "Happy Birthday," shovel treats, and tell the new UPS person that you have no clue where the address is that he is looking for (even if it's yours and he is bringing you a check for one million dollars from Publisher's Clearing House). If there is room for you to escape—even a foot or two—do so. You can even position yourself so

Give your dog a chance to surprise you. Jolanta's dog-aggressive dog Juniper had diarrhea the other night and had to go out pronto at an unaccustomed time. Jolanta never, ever leaves the house without treats…except this time. While walking around her Brooklyn block she ran into six dogs, four of whom were unfamiliar (and thus more upsetting to Juniper) and two of whom she encountered twice because they went around the block twice. Each time Jolanta saw a dog, she moved as far away as she was able, and she talked to Juniper softly and happily and had him target to her hand over and over as they passed by. Amazingly, apart from a brief instance of staring, Juniper remained very calm the entire time.

Karen is blocking Jerome from a person who is asking directions. Note that Karen is feeding Jerome, as well as holding on to his collar. Photo by Gina Boderck.

your back is to the UPS person; don't worry about being rude. I somehow think that it would be much worse if your dog lunged at the person than if you just turned your back on him.

In either scene, remember that if your dog will still eat in these kinds of situations, you are reaping some benefit because your dog is focused on you and not the scary thing. If your dog isn't eating and is reacting, try your recall word, clapping, or having him nose target your hand. If those fail, put a wad of food in your dog's face and see if he'll eat; if so, adjust your hand so that he is looking back at you. Feeding while aggressing is

Recently at a dog show, someone recognized Shadow and me and raced up to talk just as I was leaving the ring. She crowded us both against a wall and leaned over him. I surreptitiously grabbed his collar, fed him nonstop, and insinuated myself between her and Shadow with my back to her. She may have thought me rude, but Shadow remained calm.

With all of my prep work for Shadow getting his CD (Companion Dog) title, there was one "scene" that I completely forgot to train for—after the off-leash portion and as you leave the ring, the steward brings you the leash with arm outstretched. In an instant, rather than panic, I asked Shadow to sit and stay, walked up to the steward, retrieved my leash, went back to Shadow, and clipped it on.

not my favorite idea; however, I do understand that during damage control, there may well be no other choice—we can't always have our druthers. Feeding and ultimately getting your dog's attention back on you through an aggressive response is damage control—not a plan for long-term success.

If your dog frequently goes over his threshold, you aren't likely to get very far in your desensitization and counterconditioning program. The experience is stressful to your dog. If repeated too often, it is likely to increase rather than decrease his sensitivity to certain triggers, and so you will indeed see more intense aggressive displays. The occasional episodes, while not what we want, will happen. Just remember, they are hardly ever the end of the world. Shake them off and move on.

After the crisis has passed, if your dog has been able to stay calm (or at least under control), congratulate yourself and him and go about your business, which might include deciding that this is a perfectly fine time to end your outing. Try to make sure to incorporate some fun into your walk home to get both of you as happy and relaxed as possible.

If not—if you've had a full-blown aggressive display—your next step is to help your dog get back his brain and his focus on you. Head for the nearest quiet place you can find and settle down. Do belly breathing and speak to your dog softly and slowly; stroke gently down the length of his back, smoothing his hackles, or pet him where he likes it best (unless, of course, he'll redirect toward you in this state). As soon as he is calm enough to attend to you, ask for a few behaviors that he enjoys and knows well enough to be able to perform under almost any circumstances. It doesn't matter whether these are manners behaviors, like a sit, multipurpose behaviors, like targeting, or tricks. Get him thinking and responding to you. Look for him to literally shake it off, take treats gently, and get a softer expression on his face.

Should you continue your outing or go home? That depends. Since your dog has gone over-threshold, he will be touchier than usual for a bit. In Chapter Six of the Big Book, I spoke about how long it takes for the stress hormones to go back to normal levels. If you know perfectly well that during this walk you'll encounter more situations that are at or near your dog's normal threshold, call it a day and head for home. The same goes if your own nerves are now completely shot—in that state, you won't be able to take the best possible care of your dog. Try, however, to make the walk home pleasant and relaxed to reset the emotional tone for your dog and you.

If, on the other hand, the problem encounter happened on the way to a place where your dog can relax and enjoy himself and where you know you're not likely to have any further trouble, and if you yourself feel pretty much okay, by all means go on. It'll be good for both of you to have a pleasant experience as soon as possible after the aggressive incident—if that involves some moderate exercise, so much the better to release more tension.

Depending on the severity (duration, intensity) of the display, how reactive your dog is generally, and how many over-the-top experiences you've had lately, you can expect to see your dog's behavior deteriorate a bit. For example, he may alert to his triggers from farther away than usual. There's no denying that this always hurts when you've been working hard with your dog; in my experience, though, as long as you readjust your program, most dogs recover the lost ground fairly quickly. You may find that once you've seen your dog recover from such episodes a couple of times, you yourself aren't as upset by them—and that, in turn, will help your dog bounce back as well.

DAMAGE CONTROL II: WHEN REAL CATASTROPHE STRIKES

There are catastrophes and then there are catastrophes. Some present ethical and legal problems that will not be addressed in this book: your dog inflicts a mutilating bite or seriously injures or kills another dog or animal. The catastrophes I am talking about are those that don't necessarily result in physical harm to anyone but inflict a body blow to your rehabilitation program—for instance, you have been working with your dog-aggressive dog so successfully that he is now almost completely non-reactive to dogs on the street and is even beginning to generalize a positive attitude toward strange dogs.

But one day, you're ambling down the sidewalk minding your own business when an aggressive off-lead dog comes tearing around the corner, roaring, and jumps your dog. Unsurprisingly, an altercation follows, and, also unsurprisingly, you now feel sick with anxiety every time you pass that corner (which happens to be one you can't avoid). Now your dog is erupting at distances that have been well below threshold for months, and the sight of dogs that resemble his attacker drives him wild. What do you do? The short answer is, square your shoulders and keep on plugging.

We all know that living with an aggressive dog is *tough*. When you've been working hard to improve your dog's behavior and catastrophe strikes anyway, you may feel let down by the world (or by yourself, if you had any role in the way the episode played out). You might feel put-upon on your dog's behalf (darn it, doesn't he ever get a break?) or guilty at failing to protect him, whether or not there was anything you could have done. You might feel sick at the thought of all the progress you've lost, and now you might feel anxious around things that remind you of the catastrophe.

As soon as you can, let all this go. Remember that *however much your dog has backslid, the situation would likely be far, far worse if not for the work you have already done.* Very few disasters are forever, and even if the immediate fallout is pretty bad, you and your dog can recover.

If the catastrophe resulted from your lapse in vigilance, consider why that lapse occurred. The idea isn't to blame yourself—everyone in the world makes mistakes, and, frankly, those of us who have aggressive dogs get quite enough blame and guilt, both internal and external—but to understand the situation as clearly and as dispassionately as possible so as to avoid it in future.

For example, if you are overtired, your judgment may deteriorate. A good rule of thumb is to make a strict rule for yourself: if you have had less than a minimum number of hours of sleep, always choose the more cautious option, no matter how confident you are feeling. Substituting this hard-and-fast rule for judgments about individual situations can keep your dog out of considerable trouble.

If the disaster was out of your control, as in the example of the off-leash dog charging your dog-aggressive dog, is there anything you can do to bring it more under your control? Once you and your dog have calmed down enough to be both courteous and very firm, make it clear to the other owner that he needs to keep his dog leashed or confined. If he refuses, by all means call Animal Control.

Once you can think rationally again, break down the scenario into tiny pieces. If you have the help of some friends with neutral dogs, set up similar types of situations to desensitize your dog, at least to some extent, to recover lost ground and build up your confidence. I have done this myself on many occasions. Chapter Nine in the Big Book discusses how to break down situations. Adjust the steps to fit your exact circumstances and be sure to practice exit strategies. Again, please avoid self-blame. It simply isn't possible to predict every possible contingency, and you can make yourself sick trying to do so. If you have access to a good class, weekend camp, or seminar for reactive dogs and you can afford to go, sign up now.

RECAP

❖ During damage control, think fast, feed if you must, and get outta there!

❖ Be sure that you have enough rest and are in the right frame of mind before doing a training session with your dog.

❖ Based on the behavior of your dog after an outburst, decide whether to continue your walk or pack it in and go home.

Invention Is the Better Part of Valor

IMPROVISATION

As you already know, the lucky people—those living in suburban and rural areas—can more easily set their dogs up to be under-threshold. They have more wide-open spaces where they can see the scary bad things coming and have many more options of safety zones, not the least of which is distance. You, dear City Person, get the "spontaneous Dumpster/parked car" or the "oh, look, there's a dog on the other side of that fence" options instead. You also need to develop the skills of switching gears and making the most of any opportunity that may cross your path.

You have identified your dog's trigger(s): what distances are critical, what variations (dog breed? person wearing a hat?) make matters better or worse, whether time of day matters, and so on. You have worked on your foundation behaviors in as many locations as possible. You are starting to see some progress. What are your next steps?

THE SPONTANEOUS PARKED CAR OPTION

You may have noticed, for example, that your dog-aggressive dog is tense and watchful but not out of his mind when a slow-moving older

Cecilia and Sally are on the sidewalk while Beau and I are in the street using these cars and mailboxes as "dotted line" protected contact. Photo by Gina Boderck.

dog is across the street. This is a cue to you (watchful but not over-threshold) to use this opportunity for a training session. You're out walking your dog and spot just such a candidate across the street. You were planning on going in the other direction, but now it's time to change your itinerary. Walk on your side of the street, in the same direction as the other dog. The spaces between parked cars on the street will afford your dog brief glimpses of the other dog, and during those times when he can see the other dog, you will feed him his special treats or play with him. Depending on where you are in your training, as you approach the spaces you can say, "Where's the dog?" Three minutes of this, and you have just added another below-threshold session to your piggy bank.

THE SPONTANEOUS NEUTRAL DOG ON A LEASH OPTION

Suppose you're walking along and you see a dog simply hanging out with his owner. The dog appears to be calm, and in fact when he spots you and your dog, he ignores you.

Once you are done being jealous, realize that you have the equivalent of a prepared setup with a stationary neutral dog. You can walk back and forth a few times, and then—results and safety permitting—you can gradually decrease the distance between the dogs. Again, here you can use features of the landscape as visual barriers to increase your chances of success. Be sure to watch the neutral dog for any signs of stress.

Cecilia is walking Sally, and Gina has Gus. Gus is lunging at Sally, and Gina is standing in a proper "bracing" position to hold Gus in check, so he doesn't drag her forward.

Using protected contact at a school: Jane and Ruby are outside the fence, and Karen and Takoda are inside the fence.

THE SPONTANEOUS PROTECTED CONTACT OPTION

Dog parks can provide protected contact situations for working with dog-aggressive and dog-reactive dogs. Walk past at an appropriate distance; be sure to keep your dog busy doing fun stuff and your session short.

THE SPONTANEOUSLY APPEARING XYZ OPTION

"XYZ," of course, can be anything your dog is reactive to: a shopping cart, a uniform, a bicycle. Suppose your dog is reactive to people in wheelchairs, but you don't know anyone who uses a wheelchair. If you think the time is right, utilize the person you see sitting in a wheelchair relaxing with a newspaper. Tether your dog at a distance, then approach and politely ask whether you may work with him near the person to get him over his fear of wheelchairs. Wheelchair users, in my experience, are often glad to oblige; they're well aware of how many dogs react to people in wheelchairs, and someone who's actually working on the problem is likely to be looked on favorably.

THE "CAN I COME OVER AND PLAY?" OPTION

If you have friends with a fenced yard, will they let you use it when they aren't home? Access to a safe open space will give you a little breathing room to train and play without having to constantly scan your environment. An added benefit is that you will be able to train in a novel place and thus work on your distraction training.

Another option that may be available to you is to rent a training space for an hour during off hours. This will give your dog a chance to work off leash and to build your training to a new level, as well as allowing him to run around like a maniac while you laugh hysterically at his antics. Maybe get some friends together and share the cost. Once you are safely ensconced in the room, *be sure to lock the door!*

START YOUR OWN E-MAIL LIST

You can even start your own e-mail list for people who have dogs with similar issues in your area. Members can help each other design and implement training and desensitization sessions; working together is a great way to make friends, get emotional support, and see some real progress. Perhaps local trainers would be willing to put their clients in touch with you; you could also post notices on dog-related listservs that you belong to. Members of your group should be in general agreement about methods; there's no sense in adding to your stress, and thereby to your dog's, by trying to work on counterconditioning with a partner who's delivering leash pops to her dog as you work.

CHILDREN

Reactivity to children is difficult to work on under the best of circumstances. With great caution, and depending on the degree of your dog's reactivity, you may be able to use venues such as playgrounds and schools. In deciding whether this is appropriate for you and your dog, you must always keep in mind the possible consequences. Not only is it terribly unfair to children to put them in a position to be frightened or hurt, but also a bad misstep could cost your dog his life, and you could lose your house. If you use a muzzle at no other time, this may be the situation in which you should do so.

Scout out your local playgrounds, schools, ice cream shops. How far can you stand from them and still see them? Is there a place where you can stand and be confident that you will not be blindsided by approaching children as you work with your dog? Are visual barriers available? What times are busiest and least busy? Does the sidewalk or path offer any routes for retreat?

The ideal situation is one in which:
- Your dog is aware of the children but is under-threshold.
- You can't be blindsided.
- You can close the distance somewhat as your dog progresses but always with clear lines of sight and avenues of retreat so that your dog won't be surprised into an aggressive episode by a child suddenly appearing too close by.

If you don't have all of the above requirements, then don't do a "kid" session. Period. More than in any other work with reactive dogs, it's crucial that you be alert, calm, and well-rested. Keep sessions brief and always, always err on the side of safety.

It's also possible to work with individual children under their parents' supervision. Trust and clear communication are essential. Perhaps a friend would be willing to stand quietly with her toddler as you walk past, feeding your reactive dog and keeping him busy, twenty feet away. Older children, again under their parents' supervision, can be asked to do things such as ride a skateboard slowly past at an appropriate distance. Jolanta has worked with mildly reactive dogs on her block by sitting with the dog on her porch as children play on the dead-end street. One person can body-block the steps while a second carries out desensitization exercises.

Working with a reactive or aggressive dog in the city can be stressful and alienating, but it can also be surprisingly rewarding. Success is greatly enhanced by your relationships with your neighbors and even with the people you casually run into. Needing to be spontaneous and alert is difficult, but it also makes you a flexible and clever trainer. And, finally, you can't beat the sheer number of reps possible when you live in a city. On any reasonably nice day, you can likely count on seeing half a dozen to a dozen dogs during a forty-five-minute walk. If you stay focused and use each of those encounters as an opportunity to work with your dog, that's as much practice as a person in the country may be able to get in a solid week.

● **RECAP**

❖ *Be creative!*
❖ *Be fast on your feet!*
❖ *Be safe!*
❖ *Find like-minded friends and practice together.*

Appendix 1

Please feel free to make copies of these pages. These lists may help you until being creative and unpredictable are as easy as breathing. Cut them up into little strips and put them in a separate box marked for each kind of list (reinforcers, foundation behaviors, and new behaviors). Pull a few slips out from each box for every training session, and that is how you will reinforce and what behaviors you will practice.

List of Suggested Reinforcers

Feel free to add in your own—be creative and watch your dog to see what floats his boat.

- A wad of treats, all fed one at a time
- Throw food up in the air while cheering
- Clapping
- Cheering
- Soft petting
- Rough petting
- Blow bubbles
- Go sniff
- Sniff the food

* Tease with toy
* Play with toy
* Pluck grass or snow and throw up in the air
* Run around silly
* Go swimming
* Hand targeting
* The chance to do a favorite pet trick
* Allow dog to play with a special friend (human or dog)

List of Foundation Behaviors
A few of these should be practiced at each training session.

* Bridge response
* Eye contact
* Name response
* Heel with attention
* Accepting tactile
* Accepting of secondary reinforcers
* Stays
* Come
* Door etiquette
* Crate training
* Trading (not being possessive about objects/people/locations)

List of New Behaviors to Train During a Training/Desensitization Session
Pick one or two per session. If the behavior is very complicated, then only pick one to train at a time.

* Retrieve an object
* Jumping through a hoola hoop or over a jump

- ✲ Moving stand
- ✲ Sit
- ✲ Down
- ✲ Stay
- ✲ Shake paw
- ✲ Hand signals for sit and down
- ✲ Spinning to the right and left
- ✲ Weaving in between your legs
- ✲ "Clean up" – putting toys in basket on cue
- ✲ Rollover
- ✲ Settle
- ✲ Bow
- ✲ Agility obstacles (tire, table, tunnel, weaves, teeter, A-frame, dog walk, chute, jumps)
- ✲ Riding a skateboard
- ✲ Balancing on a board with a tennis ball nailed to the bottom of it
- ✲ Tracking—finding the person whose scent "pad" he has sniffed or even just following a scent of liver that you dragged along the ground
- ✲ "Wipe your feet" (on a towel or mat)
- ✲ Wagging his tail on cue
- ✲ Closing a door
- ✲ Ringing a bell
- ✲ Picking a sock that has your scent on it from a pile of otherwise clean socks
- ✲ Finding your keys
- ✲ Automatic sits with continued focus when you stop moving
- ✲ Right turns and left turns
- ✲ About turns
- ✲ Stand for exam (on ground or on table)
- ✲ Drop on recall
- ✲ Drop as he is running away from you

- Call front
- Instant down
- Fast and slow pace
- Directionals
- Coming away from the other dogs in your household
- Accepting of muzzle
- "Go visit"
- Nose target your hand
- Find a treat or toy under a towel or blanket

Sample Log Sheet

Date: _5/10/04_ Location: _Walking on the trail_

Context: (describe in detail) _One person and dog in front of us and one person and dog behind us, both at a 30-foot distance_

Number of minutes: _10 minutes—5 minutes out and 5 minutes back_

Rate the behaviors practiced from 1-5, 5 being great:

Note: "X: means we didn't practice that behavior.

_3_ eye contact _5_ name recognition _3_ heeling with attention

_5_ come response _5_ sit _5_ down _X_ stay _4_ basic attention

_5_ door etiquette _5_ crate training _2_ accepting tactile

__ other behaviors (describe) _threw a toy and played fetch_

Reinforcers used: _Food, petting, pet tricks, petting, toss the stick_

Any reaction? Describe in detail: _His door etiquette coming out of the van was perfect. From the van to the trail, I let him get ahead of me by a few feet and practiced calling him back. He was successful each time (4 times). Lots of good smells today and his attention could have been better. He kept looking back at the person and dog following us in a sort of nervous way, but there was no aggressive reaction. There was a jogger that went by, so we ran off into the woods and I fed him while the jogger passed. I tried to use petting as a reinforcer, but sometimes he avoided it._

LOG SHEET

Date:_____ Location:_____

Context: (describe in detail)_____

_____

_____

_____

_____

Number of minutes:_____

Rate the behaviors practiced from 1-5, 5 being great:

___eye contact ___name recognition ___heeling with attention

___come response ___ sit ___down ___stay ___basic attention

___door etiquette ___crate training ___accept tactile

__other behaviors (describe)_____

_____

Reinforcers used: _____

Any reaction? Describe in detail: _____

_____

_____

_____

_____

_____

_____

_____

_____

_____

LOG SHEET FOR YOUR HELPER

This is a great way to evaluate how your sessions are going. It is very often hard to remember exactly what you did during a session because you were busy trying not to hyperventilate. A valuable tool would be to have someone to watch and record for you the following questions:

HOW MANY DIFFERENT BEHAVIORS DID YOU SEE?

What were they?_____

Did you see any foundation behaviors being practiced?_____

What were they?_____

Did you see any new behaviors being practiced?_____

What were they?_____

How many different types of reinforcers did you see used?_____

What were they?_____

Did you see any calming/stress signals?_____

What were they?_____

Did you see any progress in the session?_____

What was it?_____

What needs work?_____

BREAKDOWN OF MY DOG'S ISSUES

This sheet should be filled out at the beginning of your training and then again every six months to go along with your log sheets. Knowing exactly what triggers your dog to react or aggress is the first step in helping him. This will help you see progress and what you still need to work on. If you need more room or have different issues than listed below, add to the bottom of the form. Be sure to keep it simple and make it easy on yourself—you don't need full sentences. Be sure to define the distance for each of these things, as well as duration (how long he can be in the presence before aggressing.)

MY DOG'S ISSUES

Date:_____

Things my dog aggresses at: ___Men ___Women ___Kids (define—ages, walking, running, on bikes or skateboards, swimming, playing)_____

___Men in hats ___Men with beards ___One person alone

___Groups of people ___ Eye contact from strangers

___Moving body parts ___Direct contact

___Grooming (define) _____

___ People walking ___ People running/jogging

___ People coming up from behind ___ Mail or UPS person

___ People on the other side of a fence or barrier

Other _____

___Direct eye contact from a dog

___Certain breed(s) of dogs (list)_____

___Male dogs (intact/neutered) ___Female dogs (intact/spayed)

___Dogs running ___Dogs walking ___Dogs playing ___Dogs coming up to the crate ___Dogs approaching head on ___Dogs sniffing his hind end

___On leash __Off leash ___Puppies

Other_____

Inanimate objects: ___Coats ___Sunglasses ___Hats ___Gloves ___Boots

___Umbrellas ___Playground equipment ___Stuffed animals ___Drainpipes

___Manhole covers ___Papers blowing in the wind ___Loud noises

___Trucks ___Water (bath, lake or river) ___Gravel ___Ice ___Pots and pans dropping ___Thunder___Shopping carts ___Loud music

Other_____

Appendix 2
Additional Resources

READING LIST

Training

Bones Would Rain From the Sky, by Suzanne Clothier

Bringing Light to Shadow: A Dog Trainer's Diary, by Pamela Dennison

Calming Signals, On Talking Terms with Dogs (video and book), by Turid Rugaas

Clicker Training for Obedience: Shaping Top Performance Positively (for competition), by Morgan Spector

Click Your Way to Rally Obedience, by Pamela Dennison

Coercion and Its Fallout, by Murray Sidman

The Complete Idiot's Guide to Positive Dog Training, by Pamela Dennison

Conquering Ring Nerves: A Step-by-Step Program for All Dog Sports, by Diane Peters Mayer, MSW

Culture Clash, by Jean Donaldson

Excel-erated Learning, by Pamela Reid

How Dogs Learn, by Mary Burch and Jon Baily

How to Meditate with Your Dog: An Introduction to Meditation for Dog Lovers, by James Jacobson and Kristine Chandler Madera

Learning and Behavior, by Paul Chance

Mine, by Jean Donaldson

On Aggression, by Konrad Lorenz

That Winning Feeling, by Jane Savoie
The Other End of the Leash, by Patricia McConnell
Why Zebras Don't Get Ulcers, by Robert Sapolsky

Health

The Holistic Guide for a Healthy Dog, by Wendy Volhard and Kerry Brown
Dr. Pitcairn's Complete Guide to Natural Health for Dogs and Cats, by
    Richard H. Pitcairn and Susan Hubble Pitcairn
Give Your Dog a Bone or Grow Your Pups with Bones, by Ian Billinghurst

WEBSITES

General Book Resources—sites where you can order the books listed above

www.dogwise.com

www.amazon.com

www.sitstay.com

Behavior and Training—sites where you can learn more about behavior and training

http://www.dogexpert.com/Polsky%20Papers/Electronicfences.html

http://www.wagntrain.com/OC/

http://employees.csbsju.edu/tcreed/pb/operant.html

http://employees.csbsju.edu/tcreed/pb/pavcon.html

http://www.flyingdogpress.com/

http://www.vin.com/VINDBPub/SearchPB/Proceedings/PR05000/PR00312.htm

http://www.bcrescuetexas.org/Training/DESENSITIZATION%20AT%20THE
    %20VET%20CLINIC.doc

Miscellaneous

Pam Dennison—*Information on training, health, vaccination protocols, car sickness info, recipes, an e-mail list and Camp R.E.W.A.R.D. for aggressive dogs.*

www.positivedogs.com

TTouch—*Information about the Tellington TTouch*
http://www.lindatellingtonjones.com/ttouch.shtml

Clicker Solutions—*A great resource for articles*
http://www.clickersolutions.com/index.html

Stacy Braslau-Schneck—*Another great source for articles*
http://www.wagntrain.com/OC/

Competing at Your Peak—*For performance anxiety*
www.competingatyourpeak.com

TRAINING TOOLS

I am sure you noticed in this book that I don't mention "tools" other than a flat buckle collar or harness and a long line. The following are my favorite places to get these things:

The X-Back Sledding Harness
 Black Ice Dog Sledding (item #HS52)—www.blackicedogsledding.com. Phone: 320-485-4825. Go to their website and look for the instructions on how to measure for a harness. Measure TWICE, order once. This harness is not adjustable.

Leather Tracking Harnesses (Padded Breastplate)—
 This is my other pick for a harness. Use this if your dog tends to back out of collars or if he is the size of a big Lab or German Shepherd. He won't be able to get out of this tracking harness. The harnesses are beautifully made, comfortable, and fully adjustable. You can get them from:

 Leerburg Training Equipment—(padded leather agitation harness, item #799-1) http://leerburg.com/799.htm

 K9 Solutions—(leather agitation harness, item #233) https://www.dope-dog.com/store/customer/product.php?productid=233&cat=36&page=1

Elite   K9—(3-point, leather agitation harness, item   #AH-03M) http://www.elitek9.com/Harnesses/index.htm

Leashes

BridgePortEquipment.com—They have the best leashes. For the 33-foot long lines (leather and nylon), go to the tracking section. I use the 3/8" or the 1/2" wide. When buying a long line, don't get cotton—it rots and breaks at the worst possible moment!

About the Author

Pamela S. Dennison

Pam's work with aggressive dogs started when she adopted a one-year-old Border Collie named Shadow. Unbeknownst to her, she had a human-aggressive dog on her hands. It was through her work with Shadow that she was able to gain the observational and training skills necessary to work with aggression. In a mere eighteen months, Pam took Shadow from being a human-aggressive dog to one able to earn his Canine Good Citizen certificate and subsequent Rally Championship title (ARCH), RL3, CD, NA, NAJ, TSW.

Pam has been training dogs since 1992 and started her own business, Positive Motivation Dog Training, in 1997. She teaches puppy kindergarten, beginners, Canine Good Citizen, musical Freestyle, Rally, and competition classes at her facility in Belvidere, New Jersey. She works with every breed, from Dachshunds to Great Danes to every size in between, on a myriad of behavioral issues. Pam holds behavior modification classes for aggressive and reactive dogs based on her work with Shadow, as well as seminars and camps (Camp R.E.W.A.R.D.).

Pam started competing in 1996 and qualified and competed in the Eastern United States Dog Obedience Championships in 1997. After switching to positive training methods from traditional, punishment-based ones, she started her own school in 1997. At present she lives with three rescued dogs, all Border Collies. Her dogs

Photo by Louis Ruediger.

have earned many titles to date, spanning Competition obedience, Rally obedience, and agility. Pam continues to compete for more titles in these sports, as well as training for sheepherding, tracking, carting, and water sports. To date, her students have earned a multitude of titles and certificates in obedience, Rally, tracking, sheepherding, Canine Good Citizen, and Therapy Dog programs.

Pam is the author of *The Complete Idiot's Guide to Positive Dog Training* (Alpha Books), *Bringing Light to Shadow: A Dog Trainer's Diary* (Dogwise Publishing), *How to Right a Dog Gone Wrong: A Roadmap for Rehabilitating Aggressive Dogs* (Alpine Publications) and *Click Your Way to Rally Obedience* (Alpine Publications). Pam also has two videos available, *Camp R.E.WA.R.D. for Aggressive Dogs* and *Positive Solutions for Standard Behavioral Problems* (both from Barkleigh Productions). Pam is a member of the APDT (Association of Pet Dog Trainers), the NADOI (National Association of Dog Obedience Instructors), and the DWAA (Dog Writers Association of America). She is also a Certified Dog Behavior Consultant with the IAABC (International Association of Animal Behavior Consultants).

Pam has published articles in the *Blairstown Press*, *The Clicker Journal*, various BowTie publications, *Chronicle of the Dog* (APDT newsletter), and *Dog Sport Magazine*, and is the training writer for the New England Border Collie Rescue newsletter, *Have You Herd?* She has been a regular presenter at various venues, speaking on a variety of topics relating to positive training and aggression. Pam also has worked closely with Sussex County Friends of Animals and Pet Adoption League and developed a retraining program for shelter dogs.

Jolanta Benal, CPDT

In 2002, Jolanta found that she had adopted a dog-aggressive puppy and that the usual guides for working with reactive and aggressive dogs didn't always apply well to the dense urban environment where she lives. As an outgrowth of learning how best to help her dog, she became a professional trainer and now teaches manners classes and works with private behavioral clients in New York City.

Photo by Sarah M. Egan.

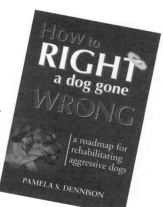

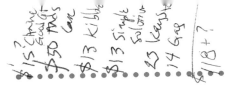

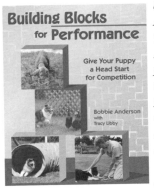